The Love Sheet

The Love Sheet

Barbara Fairhead & Jacques Coetzee

First published by Hands-On Books 2017
PO Box 121, Rondebosch, 7701, Cape Town, South Africa

info@modjajibooks.co.za

© Barbara Fairhead and Jacques Coetzee

ISBN (print): 978-1-928215-50-9
ISBN (ebook): 978-1-928215-52-3

Cover design by Megan Ross
Cover artwork by Lauren Smith
Production by Fire and Lion

Contents

The Long-Dreamed Dream   1

Shipwrecked   2

Soft Rain   3

Apocalypse   4

Song for the Duende   5

I Have Prepared for Winter   6

The Love Sheet   7

Dusky Song   8

The Journey   9

The Question   11

The Cry   12

Faith   14

I Fall Into His Face   15

The Flashlight of the Mind   16

The Mating   17

The Madness of Growing Things   18

Casa Milagro   19

Symposium   21

Brief History   22

Dark Place   23

Leaving the World   24

The Silence of Trees   25

Sleep   26

Heretic Sky   27

For a Young Poet   28

Fugitive   29

Contract   30

Beyond Our Means   32

A Future Memory   33
Commitment Ceremony   34
The Matrix   36
House of Loveliness   38
Howl   39
The Rim   40
For Jacques   41
The Slow Art   43
At the Edge of Myself   44
The Sound of Distance   46
Edges   47
Descent   49
Bridges   50
Turning-Point   51
From Across the Room   52
Stripped Down   54
Rage   55
A Thing Apart   57
Full-Moon Vigil   58
Tides   59
Death by Moon   61
Stillness   63
A New Voice   64
Wind Chime   65
Haiku   66
Haiku   66
Haiku   66
The Apprenticeship   67
Fragment   68
What We Live By   69

Late Summer 70

Shards 71

The Road Heads East 72

Singing-Bowl 74

The River Beneath the River 75

Wild Place 76

Haiku 77

Haiku 77

Haiku 77

Clock Time 78

Tokai 79

Autumn Drive 80

Your Bright Future 81

Switch 82

Ode to Mystery 83

The Inner Work 85

Stone Cottage: West Coast 87

Happy 88

Afterword 91

The Long-Dreamed Dream

They found the sheaf of love poems
after she died:

a fair armful it was;

and were amazed to learn
that their mother,
always so circumscribed
in matters of the heart,
so far beyond such yearnings,

had glimpsed
—somewhere between
the never-ending daily chores
and the long-dreamed dream—

the young lover
waiting
on Ithaca's breathless shores.

B. F.

Shipwrecked

Today I assert nothing:
no thing obeys my call.
Today I am a shipwrecked sailor,
panting on a beach in blinding sunlight:
bruised, battered, but alive.

I am the shipwrecked lover of the world,
panting naked on the shores of wonder

without words, without a song to my name—

only a steep dirt road before me
and the thin rope of my astonishment.

J. C.

Soft Rain

What I remember of the day:
soft rain;
and the touch of our fingertips' shy coupling...
and the sweet intimacy of our pilgrimage
over broken ground
and the way you listened
with your body leaning into my voice
and hearing
so deeply
far deeper than words
the tender heart-beat of unspoken things.

B. F.

Apocalypse

It isn't always like they told us:
fanfare of trumpets, white light, catastrophe.
Sometimes there is this soft
leap beyond the self, beyond
the counting of old scores

into a room that's open to the sky,
into another. So that
the soul, counting its scars out of habit,
wakes up surprised
at some perfect sunrise, much later,
and finds that it remembers
how to be happy.

J. C.

Song for the Duende

Some of us will take
our passion to the grave
and terrify the angels
with its fire
and love fiercely
this new wild dance
and dazzle death
with raw duende song.

Not for us the long sleep,
nor the gentle rock and lull
of eternity's equilibrium,
but wildness—
set free at last.

So that
—abandoning all restraint—
we shall spread time out
like a love-sheet
whereon to know all pleasures—

until the gods themselves
stand back amazed
at such desire.

B. F.

I Have Prepared for Winter

I have prepared for winter;
have learned the ache
of things diminished:
architecture of bare places
or things denuded, pruned
almost into nothing.

What then is this
voluptuous and lush
trembling of the seven senses
into—delight,
into this startling sorrow,
this terrible and inappropriate
fire?

J. C.

The Love Sheet

Free of all limitations we may serve,
the love sheet spreads itself on broken ground,
and summons to the core of its design
our restless souls.

Nor does it fear the monstrous tread of time,
but gathers in the night, the wind, the stars
that such as we may truly comprehend
the character of fate.

Nor will the cost be less,
for those who dare these shores,
than everything.

And we will find, at last
(cast up on virgin land,
washed clean by oceanic tide and time)
our commingled souls,
simple as a woven, bleach-white linen sheet—
haunted by wind.

B. F.

Dusky Song

Tonight is made for dusky songs,
for all things half-done, in between:
the dance half-danced, the sentence
that hangs in the frosty air
waiting for your voice to complete it.

You know how it is:
we have stood on the edges of ourselves—and leapt;
and still we are where we always were.

But words are too brittle to carry this knowing.
Let this at least be finished:
tonight, in Rumi's field of wine-drenched hearts,
I shall plant for us
a secret, unnamed, many-branching tree.

J. C.

The Journey

This face
that looks out from the sepia photograph,
eyes on some distant country
—as yet but one of dreams—
holds for me a haunting.

It seems a thousand ships sail through the portals of
        those eyes;
and some longed-for Ithaca floats in that soft gaze
—lies in the half-smile—
and she dreams a distant harbour, veiled
by salt of island mist
and haze.

It is as if she held the knowledge of distant lands,
of a journey
and the certainty of its attainment
within her hands.

I am twice her age now,
close to that journey's end,
and I have learned to harness disappointment:
to make of disillusionment a painful friend.

And I have learned to pray—

↘

and come to know
—how strange it seems—
that the world is
—and is not—
the dream.

B. F.

The Question

Who are we when we close our eyes?
That's still the only question worth our trouble.
Go and read the holy books: you'll find
the burden of their song
is nothing more than its slow framing.

You find as you grow older
nothing reflects your true face any more.

Yesterday, out of old memory,
a song drifted up, a parable:
a woman breaks a mirror bit by bit,
a lying image. It will not tell her
who she is. I picture her there
after the triumphant chorus fades:

shards of glass in her hands, an empty frame
to fill with a new, terrifying question.

J. C.

The Cry

It was a cry
—sudden as light—
that leapt
through the wide-flung shutter
of broken sight, to fly
unbound:

a cry that kept resounding
through each vibrating cell,
long after time returned
and flesh was still.

It was a cry that woke her again in the night,
that flew the darkness like a small, swift bird
—urgent in flight—
released at last from broken lips:
a clear, clean note.

A cry
so new—
so newly born—
this new-born thing:

a cry
unloosed,
unleashed
to fly
—astonished by lightness—
impalpable as light.

B. F.

Faith

After a lifetime's journey, there is this
shaking voice that breaks
through: to have lived by the faith
that the interior world is larger

than all of outer space,
and then to have it proven
now
by the sound of your own voice,
shaking like a forest swept by wind—
do you hear it?—the immense shudder
that tells you that you are
finally
grounded.

J. C.

I Fall Into His Face

The late afternoon light, tender as last-love,
throws a bridge from winter into spring;
slants across the empty room, the littered table where we sit,
and falls upon the story of his face:
a strong face, lit by this single shaft—
sudden as sunlight in an empty church.

It falls upon the forehead's generous plane,
the dark line of the brow; the shadowed eyes;
the unblinking gaze.

He leans into my voice
and listens
—the way wild things attend their world—
a quality of listening, palpable in its intensity.

I allow the dark angel to take me over that sensuous edge.
I enter his world of erotic sensitivity:

I fall into the invitation of parted lips
that speak of introspection,
of moral fortitude,
and wilful humour.

I fall into the clean honesty of character.
I fall into his face.

B. F.

The Flashlight of the Mind

And if now
by the flashlight of the mind
I was to look for you,
conjure you as I have come to know you,
you would split into a thousand points of memory,
disjointed bits unable to cohere.

But if I sweep these aside and wait
in the rich, silent dark, and listen,
forgetting what I am listening for,
in that empty space I have made ready
I know that you will always meet me—
a whole presence that can extinguish me
and give me back
to the generous dark.

J. C.

The Mating

You have written a song of love in Braille upon my heart—
and there, for all time, it shall be.

For with your song, I feel you
—fierce and passionate as a storm-wind—
enter me—
and I become the storm-tossed forest
and each lovely, consummated tree;

and, wild and wind-tossed, feel my very roots stir
in the dark and loamy earth—
and the madness of that wild sap rising—
rising to meet you.

B. F.

The Madness of Growing Things

I want to learn the madness
of things that grow in the ground out of doors:
I have heard them dance in the midst
of winds that would destroy them,
and I believe that they put out each spring
new, fragile leaves in foolhardiness.

I do not want to hear histories of old wrongs,
to tease out arguments like rats' tails.
I want to taste the stubborn madness of trees
that grow on down into the mad,
unreasoning, receptive earth.

J. C.

Casa Milagro

Today there is no wind.

I listen to the resonance
of your voice,
your song,
and hear it fly
out across this silent land—
a desert hawk,
dark against the desert sky;
and watch it skim
the long,
long sweeping curve
of a soft horizon's rim.

Today there is no wind;
the sky is full of blue—

and I listen to the desert
breathing in
the resonance of this song,
breathed out by you
a lifetime ago,
and on a distant shore,

yet echoes here in silent rock
and the mesa's shadowed fall,
and in my heart—a resonance
evermore.

Today there is no wind;
the sky is full of blue—
and I am breathing you.

B. F.

Symposium

At the conference centre for the blind that day,
for once, I had the advantage:

they sat us down around the table,
then turned out the lights.

I could hear the darkness everywhere:
disembodied voices unfurled
and took the air like tremulous birds

in sudden urgency. I could feel the mixing
of panic and wonder in each sighted body
searching for recognition, for a mirror
in the invisible faces all around.

And it was in that instant our hands met
as if for the first time—
two children in a dark room,
the world big and urgent outside,
speaking the word "trust" for the first time.

J. C.

Brief History

We ran into the night, you and I,
like children in a fairy-tale
running into wonder.

Some might laugh at such improvidence;
might shake a knowing head, and smile;
might offer prudent counsel.

A child knows better what it needs
than these; has not yet learned to shame
the mercy of foolish acts.

And so we made the night our own,
and strange
and beautiful;
and listened to the starlight together,
and the wind

and gave no thought to distant dawn,
but lived the fullness of this once
and only night—
into our brief history.

B. F.

Dark Place

To have worked myself into this dark place,
because some inner eye in me
had started to focus;

to have been compelled to find
the deepest watering-place;

to have come barefoot
and without expectations—

and then to find you in the palpable dusk,
to let my weary hands and knees go down
and to plunge my head again and again
into that sweetness
until there's nothing to be known,
and the mind shuts itself up in ecstasy.

J. C.

Leaving the World

I wanted to show you a world of mist and mountain:
wanted you to feel that silence;
to take you far from streets and houses and small rooms—
from the smallness of all that was familiar.

And so we left behind all conversation,
and sat together beyond the tidy world,
while the mist rolled down its veils of silence
into a place made mute by whiteness.

We uttered no word.
And I watched the slow wonder light your face;
and the wetness
breathe a film of stars into your hair.

And you were all there was that day of blood and bone—
and the white mist around you.

B. F.

The Silence of Trees

Each time, one step before I touch them,
I am aware of the trees.
Like this, in the dark, how long would it take
to learn a forest like a poem, by heart?

The trees say nothing.
With my extended left arm I find them:
every ten paces, except here and there
where one has fallen.

Against one I press a stubbly cheek,
my cool wonder touching the rough bark;
then, right arm loosely linked with yours, we walk.
Beneath my sandaled feet the earth crunches:
needles lie over dead leaves
in a long, slow decay.

I remember our hands meeting, skin against skin,
the sun setting on our backs—
breathing so easily
with the wide and hollow earth beneath our feet.
Upright or lying down, dead or alive,
it has room enough for all of us.

And still the trees say nothing.

J. C.

Sleep

The air around your sleeping form is like a veil
through which I dare not put my hand—
but stand in awe, as at the edge of some vast desert,
silent and inscrutable—immense beyond imagination.

The solitude that surrounds you is like the silence
           around a stone.

One does not enter such a land.
Nor does one violate that subtle wall—fierce,
even in its stillness.

On what ancient tides do you offer up
the pilot of your will,
to sail—astonished—
the anarchy of dreams?

On what uncharted seas
does the animal-you set loose
its storm of curbed and bridled hungers?

And what is the nature of that vessel
to which you give your trust, night after night,
so wantonly—
certain of your safe return?

B. F.

Heretic Sky

I want to eat my bread with heretics,
with those who can never fully enter
the sanctuary of any city,
but make their bed out in some open ground—
a tent into which naked earth and sky
can reach their silent wonder.

I want to eat my bread with those
who can slip into the silence of themselves
where the world can never follow, unless there be
one pilgrim who will take that road,
and pitch a tent at a respectful distance
under a wondrous, still, heretic sky.

J. C.

For a Young Poet

I shall not see you grow old.
That will not be part
of this love's consummation.

Yet, there is a tradition of long standing;
of workmanship undertaken for its own joy.

The men of old laboured a lifetime, yet never saw
the cathedral standing proud upon the cornerstone
they laid—
nor could they but dream its greatness.

I will live this day to the full:
lay it well, this cornerstone
of love, and make no place
for sadness or regret.

For the gift of such a love, it is not seemly
to argue the price; and you will always be for me
the youthful lover, dreamer, poet, friend,
singing your way into life: and the road ahead
of you—to your particular greatness—
an open invitation to wonder.

R. F.

Fugitive

You are beautiful today
moving unseen by me in the next room
paying attention to the things you do

so fugitive beauty is
hiding far from our clutter
that I will smile to myself
maybe fifty years from now
in a room somewhere or out in the sun
thinking how it had to be this way
scribbling this day and its beauty for you
paying attention in the next room
in the next body
when we were already late to get somewhere

scribbling it behind time's back
against the years and the clutter.

O borrowed beauty, stay with me this night

J. C.

Contract

I

This naked face, with the raw landscape of its biography
etched upon it, stares back at me—confused;
confused by the contradiction of inner voice and outer image;

confused to see the deep-etched, ruthless scrawl
of fine notation; a commentary once so faint
we could pretend its absence, yet now has overwritten
youth's immortality with new instruction;
has written in the small print of its contract,
and the certainty of endings.

II

You stand behind me while I do my hair.
You kiss my neck—your face so smooth,
so barely marked by history, that we
may yet ignore the fleeting shadows
yet to be crafted into flesh. And you,
who cannot read this image in the glass, or how
its text is made more shocking by your presence,
may still ignore the elegies written on it.

III

What new eyes must I now acquire
to see beneath this stranger's consternation?

What manner of sightedness makes beautiful
the indelible fingerprints of time,
the way deep water-courses, or weathered rock,
or eroded landscapes lost of their innocent bloom
gain our respect?

B. F.

Beyond Our Means

You say that time is short.

But what time could be long enough
for us who love so far beyond our means?

Come, look away from the faces of clocks
that curdle desire and make us add up the years.
Everyone knows that the stars are bright
because they go dark by day;
and that a thousand years from now
we will laugh just like this, and burn
the same brief, spendthrift candle at both ends.

J. C.

A Future Memory

What has happened to the shape of years—
those vast paragraphs of time,
that slow page by page unfolding?

Where now that story
that is always at the beginning;
that story which now—suddenly, it seems—
has lost its thread, its nerve?

Now, it seems, the future rushes in
with such unseemly haste
that the days and pages blur as they turn.
Past and future are one now,
and I see the road only when I look back.

And yet—
I see you walking down a tree-shaded street
to a road that opens like a hand—
and I am not there.

You stop, the dog beside you.
You turn your head and listen, with that faint smile
I never could decipher with any accuracy.

Your answer—
it always took me by surprise.

B. F.

Commitment Ceremony

I

Back home after a long time—
at this table, getting closer to
what I don't understand, cannot explain.

Sit here long enough, and outward things
begin to fall away: like my own voice
saying "I"; like the reasons I've made up
for being or not being here. Until, slowly, as always,
your voice comes through, emerges
like music, flowing between the stars.

II

This is a place that knows me well,
to which I find my way back always—
in the end. With this strong table between us,
the faint sounds of our writing in the background,

there is no world. There is only this slow emptying out
into a clear space where we make our stand:
listening into each other, till we find
what we could never hope for—
a recognition: always apart,
always together.

Knotted together by the same longings,
the same fierce rollercoaster of desire,
we will leave this room together, and return
to the old world of certainties. As we get up,
my arm brushes something, and the gong
you placed against the wall reverberates.
We laugh, almost in unison.

And still our fierce hearts want more; are unappeased.

J. C.

The Matrix

This year I took a fateful step out of the matrix
and, with the turning of my face, shattered
the remnants of that constricting mould.

I took a step out of the house that has grown me:
that house of orthodoxy which, however elegant its desire
to protect its own, ultimately destroys us.

I stepped out of that garden with its famous tree—for no free
            wind
may blow within its high-walled acreage. And now
I step over that terrifying and beckoning edge
—and fall

into the dark song of a half-forgotten woman;
the fierce and sudden heat of her;
and the lonely scent of wild.

I do not have the words for her song—
that ancient longing that murmurs
just beneath the threshold of memory.

But I have the breathing of it—

a sweet breath that breathes me:
pink tongue panting;
animal eyes, lazy as dreaming, and slit-lidded
against the glare of heat and thorn—

a sleek animal,
naked;
female
(with the blood-heat on her)
stalking the black wind.

B. F.

House of Loveliness

Autumn suits us this year:
living in a house full of loveliness
that took a lifetime's gathering.

We need fewer words now to say
the same things: we have grown fluent
with each other; we have grown

in secret. Seeds stir in us, sap quickens
somewhere, in secret. Whose are these many voices
that babble inside us when we are silent?

You bustle close by
in the body next to mine—invisibly.

In this house full of loveliness
there is room enough for wonder. Each time
we turn our listening bodies towards each other,
the wind turns differently in the chilly sky.

J. C.

Howl

So how can it be that I, a wolf
(skilled in solitude and high, thin places)
should now so tremble for the sweetness of your embrace;

that the memory of you, your voice, your song,
should now so resonate within me
—a resonance that haunts me to the bone?

That this shudder of wind
—that strips my heart of all its shadows,
that strips me bare of all that splendid isolation—
is come at last, fierce and ruthless,
so that I stand naked as desire,
so that all winds may find me.

Yet, I long only to surrender that solitude;
to leave those isolated wastes, and
—terrified by beauty, and the wonder of it—
offer to you the most precious thing I own:

the raw,
unguarded
and uncorrupted howl of my love.

B. F.

The Rim

I am a dancer on the rim
of knowledge. See, the dark that's ahead—
it has no bottom. It beckons

I don't know where to. But I do know
the exultation when the earth is
split open like a ripe
and fragrant fruit, when it is
naked and close like a lover,

and dangerous. I am the dancer on the rim
of the great wound love gives us,
and my secret laughter startles
the constellations into song.

J. C.

For Jacques

How may I be a pair of eyes for you—this day of days?

Last night's full moon has pulled the slow tide far from shore,
and the sea is small
and distant.

I cannot see the water's edge,
or where the meeting is of sand and wave,
or how these two invite the ocean's turning—
for the morning light has written out such things.

Now there is only this reach of naked sand—
a wet and sensuous memory of sea,
a shining band—that almost blinds the eyes;
that carries on for miles and miles along the coast,
a blessed emptiness.

There is no wind.
The sky, washed clean of blue,
does not intrude;
and all the world's horizon—soft;
a wide-brim, open bowl of invitation.

Only the static presence of the gulls
brings punctuation to the day.

↘

They stand (not quite in silhouette)
dark characters, scattered on the empty page
—all facing east—
a ritual pause;

and scribed in cuneiform (or some such ancient script)
on twin stilt legs, so straight and fine,
mirrored in wetness;
or carved (perhaps from wood)
and painted white and black in replicate design,
pretending to be real,

but still—
and silent—
and waiting—

like so many commas and semi-colons
bringing pause
to the poet's day.

B. F.

The Slow Art

This living, this dying with open eyes
is a high-stakes game: stalking
the moment from behind
to pin it down. This was the faith we lived by,
leaning for warmth into
projected futures only we could see.

How could we forget
the slipperiness of this tilting earth?
We crouch here, you and I,
more awake than we have ever been,
and still it is not enough: behind us
moments come fast and pass through,
pass through into futures never dreamed by us.

This is the slow art we learn at last:
to trace in characters of flesh and blood
the outer limits of those endless
and irreversible woundings.

J. C.

At the Edge of Myself

And now, alone and at the edge of myself,
only this tenuous, vibrating chord
—this heart-held resonance—
connects me to you:

this desire,
this slender and impossible thread of longing,
subtle and insubstantial
like a prayer breathed into the wind—

this is what I have;
this is what I hold to.

And now, night opens to me its branches of stars
and draws a ring of silence around the moon—

and I listen to the sound of distance;
to the dark silhouettes of sleeping things
—the sound of dreaming;
to fragments of memories of you.

And I long to feel the warm animal of your body
curl into the curve of me;
to breathe with you the darkness
—ever deeper—
the velvet night tasselled with dreams—

to know, again and again, that touch
(which is yours, and yours only)
that carries your voice, your song—
the all of you—

and to know with you once more
that deep—fierce—sweat-scented
—forever—
animal ecstasy.

B. F.

The Sound of Distance

In this room the sound of dusk
is a slow, muffled instrument.

In this room that almost knows me,
where I have lived for a dozen years
while my body woke and slept,
while my soul awoke and slept,
the sound of dusk has no name,

but I hear it now in the rustling of the leaves;
I feel it slip in between my footsteps;
I feel it slip in between your breasts
as you lie, a spent wave,
in the hollow of my arms

before we let the dark in;
and the world is a room we only half know,
where we lie in one another's arms, suspended—
while, out of earshot, all the world's trains whistle past.

J. C.

Edges

Always I watch the ground before your feet,
to announce to you
each faulty step and stammer
of its Braille topography;

and I see the way
each foot prepares for change—
always anticipating the unexpected.

At the head of the stairs
I watch that pause—
that moment of reckoning;
watch your foot feel its way
over that cautious edge
that separates the worlds—
see the way it turns
—the precise angle it makes—
an angle that speaks only of you.

I watch you step out into the world—
into that incomprehensible night;
step out again and again
over that blind edge of opportunity
—that ever-blind edge of the world—
with only faith to take the weight
of your uncertainty;

see those feet, drawn on
—in spite of darkness—
by some singular creature of rakish humour—
and the beckoning hand of wonder.

B. F.

Descent

I can read the signs—
these fingers tapping the table where I sit,
this mind that will not focus.
Soon it will be time again
to throw myself away.

Words form at the surface of me,
but I am already going down:
most of anyone is underground.

By day I live in a dark place;
words must be slow and few there.

My animal ears quiver upward and listen
for the sound of your footsteps,
for your clear, measured words cutting through stone.

Because of those clear words I talk with shadows;
I know that the real conversation
is always secret, always underground—
and that the world can only find us by surprise
in the deepest places, when there's no light, no sound at all.

J. C.

Bridges

As I walk with you through my sighted world,
I seek always to find a bridge to link
your world with mine. A morning mist

now shrouds the coastal hills—
those gentle, swelling curves of hip and thigh—
inviting contours of earth-flesh, so lightly veiled.
Or image now the shadows of the wind,
dark on mountain water; how they shudder
up the spine with intimations of dread;
or how the stars astound us with their brilliance—
pinpricks of shattering glass
in the vast and silent chord of night.

In your replies
I discover a world that trembles with suggestion—
a world of subtle images, held in touch, taste,
sense and sound; an erotic world
that is so close to tears and beauty
—is so immediate—that it blinds me
to the harsher edges of my seeing.

B. F.

Turning-Point

Today I want to rest
in the clear, sensual light
of all things I can touch and hear and smell—

want to feel the cool of my own shadow
that's closer to me than any sun.

Because today you stretched your hand towards me,
bridging the impossible gap between
one world and the next

so that the mad molecules that comprise me
cohered for one sane and piercing instant,
and I felt in my blood that they were beautiful.

Because of this I turn
just for this borrowed moment
my back on all things complex
(even as I smell my own close shadow)
and whisper our names back into the mystery.

J. C.

From Across the Room

Music is playing—something I recognise
from a time long gone; music that I have danced to
in my youth. The gritty scratch of dust
on ancient vinyl dates me
and the song.

From across the room I watch with fascination
the small moves your bodies make—gestures
that do not intrude in any way, or break
your concentration. And I know that you have sat,
how many times before, just so—absorbed in conversation;
will sit again, just so, long after I am gone; will play again
this dusky song.

Even from this distance I can see the film of dust
upon the piano—dust that has resisted all my efforts
with cloth and polish; dust that has filtered in
through chinks in windows, closed against the day
and the high whine of the angle grinder
from the building-site across the way.

He is reading something to you; sits sideways
on the chair, ankle across knee, shirt
unbuttoned; relaxed, unshaved, untidy hair.

You sit erect, your face raised in attention.

From time to time you throw back your head
and laugh; or smile your appreciation; or lean
forward: lean into the voice and listen—closely—so that he,
observing this, flashes you a glance—a smile
you do not see.

You raise your hands; your fingers make
swift Braille-reading gestures in the air,
perhaps to place on record something
you would remember. And then,
the slow ritual where you replace both hands on the table,
lowering each long, tapered finger
with immense care.

I watch you from across the room—
from another galaxy—
another star—

For Jacques and Henry: Stellenbosch, March 2006

B. F.

53

Stripped Down

If there was a word for it—
if there was one strong enough—
it would feel good to say it now,
to whisper it together like a talisman.

We are next to an expanse of open water;
we sit down, although we are not tired,
muffled in a total silence
that wraps itself around us
like the blanket on which we sit.

Even the weathered stone you hand me,
when questioned, says nothing;
the wind blows the water full of shadows,
symbolising nothing.

I call it all up from somewhere in my mind,
where no lens has ever entered. This is how it was:
a weathered stone, and wind on water—
your face close to mine.
If there had been a word for it,
an appropriate sign, we might have made it then—
it would have felt good
to be steadied by something there.
But there was nothing small enough to sound
in that silence.

J. C.

Rage

I will be a lioness in your corner—

or perhaps a tiger, or a hyena.
Something fierce—some primal energy that kills
without a whisker of remorse;
one that says it straight—"don't mess with me!"

—everyone needs such fierceness;

or perhaps a panther with rage in it—a clean wild rage
that cleaves the brain like a sword:
something with teeth and claws—
or a creature with two sharp tusks—
or a horn that penetrates to the bone.

It must have a fierce eye
and muscles of sprung steel;
be wired like a serpent
with energy that slices down an electric spine—
slithering—swift—lethal—connected.

And scars—
there must be scars for it to qualify—
and many years to prove its pedigree.

Above all—

it must hold the taste of blood fresh in its brain.

B. F.

A Thing Apart

I am a thing apart:
something in me resists
any hand that would reach out to know me,
even the most loving.

I wrestle with this, drink deep
to feel the forms and textures of the world
run wild and mix, as if
under an exuberant paint-brush.

And yet something inside me is always strange,
a stranger to any mixing. It knows
the wonder of tides going in and out;
holds its breath in a world
suddenly so empty, yet its own,
and the air it breathes is wild and clear
almost beyond enduring.
It does not ask for my embrace; only
that I collect myself and follow.

J. C.

Full-Moon Vigil

The night is warm. The moon
has shaped the landscape of your sleep;
has etched a long, unbroken curve
from shoulder down to toe; has lit
the contours of your sleeping form
with silence. You lie—

half-covered by the sheet, face cupped
in hand, the other by your side,
fingers mute upon your thigh—
and your close, damp curls
are dark and sudden
against white linen. How still

you lie, an alabaster faun
sculpted by moonlight—
distant as a star.

B. F.

Tides

Once I wrote a poem about the moon
moving an immensity of water
across the earth; I put that moon there for us,
an ever-changing brightness that is
somehow always new.

Now, by the sober light of day,
my own words blowing about my ears like sand,
it's hard to hear the world speak, hard
to make out the slow music of the waves;
hardest of all to follow
the unpredictable paths of my own heart.

But still, in my deepest places, I'm aware
of your words and mine as they hover—
those singing constellations—
around a silent, nameless wonder.

The music that the moon makes with the sea—
listen. It echoes through us:
your pen that moves across the page in darkness
unlocks my voice, opens my throat to sing.

In my heart now the wind has dropped;
I will wait in silence
until I catch your voice
like a key change in the music of the waves,
and the tide comes in again.

J. C.

Death by Moon

A full moon has carved your face, your form
in stone, every contour in cold white marble—
bleached white, smooth; white as weathered bone;
has written out the lines. Only this white,
white flesh—so silent, so still. The ghost

of Michelangelo might dream of this—might
envy yet the work of such a hand; might
ask what sacred muse, what light can turn
the human flesh so into stone: a reverse trick
that was, it would appear, even to that great master
a thing unsought, unattained, or else unknown.

So beautiful,
this white—
this sleeping form;
so bloodless and so still.
So relaxed the pose: no self-conscious element
informs this work of art.
No act of will.

I gaze
upon this sleeping Lazarus—his life-blood stilled—
who walks and dreams some other country,
to us unknown;

↘

waiting for day to arise this white sleep

—this momentary completion
—this death by moon.

B. F.

Stillness

And then this morning, after the wild,
passionate words, after days so full
we knew our brains had unhinged themselves
to let a whole new world in—after all that,
this morning it happened.

It was very still. The wind
had dropped down—and there we were,
just putting one foot in front of the next
as if for the first time.

You said, had I noticed how quiet it was
outside? A timeless moment,
and so ordinary; what hand
had written it while we slept
as if in water?

Such an empty world, and yet so full:
after everything, this morning
the immense stillness found and held us so—at rest.

J. C.

A New Voice

To know at last this song
breaking within me
passionate and sacred:

and the earth rushing up to meet me

and the dark ibis overhead sounding his harsh cry
calling out to me to follow:

and I
on fire
with life's discordant symmetry

–turn my face–

with its old scars
and its new bright edge

–into the uncertainty of that great wheel
–into this hard and fractured light
–into the dark wind…

B. F.

Wind Chime

I love this house, where
the lines of things have softened for me again:

dusk is a bamboo wind chime—
three notes that deepen like a pool
to dip your tired face into.

Perhaps tonight I will find music
for your words; your tongue might phrase
the mystery that finds my open throat.

Meanwhile there is dusk around us,
and this meandering train of thought,
which might as well be yours;
this chime that is content to be swayed by the wind.

Just now there is no need to strive
outwards into the sharp-edged world:
everything we need to grow is here.

J. C.

Haiku

This song that rises
out of you like clear water
from an ancient well

Haiku

Whispers in the night—
who is it speaks so softly?
Rain on a tin roof

Haiku

Sometimes it is all we have—
the ground beneath our feet—
it is enough

B. F.

The Apprenticeship

We cannot walk in one another's footsteps.
Still, of all your wanderings
perilous fragments lie open to me:
songs carved out of mountains
of silence; songs
so steep and narrow—
yet they tempt me
into this madness
of living with my heart exposed,
with the wound that never heals yet never kills me.

This I do for you, hoping
it will get easier—but it does not.
What is it makes me follow
ever deeper into this place:
fur-smell, wind-bite, silent shadows?

Only this: this undeniable
response, this voice
that longs to answer yours, this
savage, slow apprenticeship
that keeps me walking
these song-roads, heart-roads—
until my breath runs out.

J. C.

Fragment

Grief
has opened up a doorway
in my soul—

and now

you set before me
lands I dared not dream
were real.

B. F.

What We Live By

A dull week towards the beginning of winter:
puddles stand between our houses, yours and mine.

I am sitting on a couch opposite you,
speaking to no-one in particular:
tired words that have nowhere to flow,
words like standing water.

You say nothing, then slowly
place inside my hand a river stone.

It is smooth from rolling round and round
in a river you have loved and lost and loved again...

So now the world is growing dark around us,
like a strange poem that will not say what it means.
And somehow it holds clear water
flowing between us everywhere,
and we on our knees to drink it.

J. C.

Late Summer

I came upon late summer, blowing
in the corner of a far-flung field,
and marvelled that such fierce sun
yet burned in its embrace.

A wild tangle of uncut grass,
and flowers, sweet for their lateness,
surrendered their will to the lazy wind;
offered their sweetness to the day.

In such a flame,
in such desire,
what could they know
of winter?

This poem, then: a seed I place in loamy earth—
and touch with naked hands,
and fingers innocent of all design
that unseen place of silence.

I make a small hollow,
shape it to my palm,
and lay the tiny blueprint
of all that I hold holy
into its dark keeping.

B. F.

Shards

Travelling across the dark river
into this arid world,
we carry the fragments of our longing—
clear, sharp-edged and shiny—
but fragments, always.

And yet I shall sing,
shall fling a net wide to catch each broken syllable.
For this day you brought a rosary of song
on which I can thread these brittle shards of language;
I cast the net wide, till it's fit to hold
the undiluted splendours of this world.

J. C.

The Road Heads East

The road heads east, casting its thin ribbon of tar over coastal
       hills, skirting
the windswept wastes that run parallel to the sea—a fine,
       black line that travels
over desolate topography, etching into memory the longing
       for mountains.

This road has become for me a place of no dimension:
a threshold between two worlds, where the two worlds in me
       meet
and find separation. There is a point where the road turns

and leaves the sea behind—
the way a salmon turns
to face the current; turns
to swim against the river's flow; turns
and heads upstream, seeking clean, cold mountain water.

And always there comes a moment—
an instant:
some kind of crossing in my mind,
and this astonishing excitement,
this leaping of the blood that says:
"Yes!"

And then I know that I too have turned,
that I too have left the sea behind me:

and I am on a new river, old as dreaming,
and heading upstream
—breathless—

seeking a new dream—
seeking the origin of dreams—
seeking my own source.

B. F.

Singing-Bowl

For this moment only,
let it not be my voice that sings.
I want to be like that curved bowl
in another world, in a room I have called mine,
which sings into silence with many notes at the same time
because it is made of many metals, because
it shapes itself around
empty space, because it fits the cupped hand
that holds and holds it while it sings.

Struck by the mallet of the turning world,
singing or falling silent,
it is because it has made room
that it is so generously full.

J. C.

The River Beneath the River

Let us enter once more the river of old wounds—

and be amazed to find beneath its shining surface
the wide-eyed, silent fish

—drawn by urgent memory, and the fierceness of desire—

swimming upstream, steady and silver
between the dark stepping-stones of faith.

B. F.

Wild Place

At the edges of me I lean towards you:
my centre is dark to me, cloaked
in multiple layers of silence,
overwhelmed by the too-much world.

Only at this edge of me, this wild place,
from time to time a stubborn thought burns through—
felt in the mind and in the belly's hunger.

Love, this is the season of stripping down,
of opening the heart's corridors.

Lean with me into this poem, this tiny fire
on the border-line between us. Listen closely,
and you'll hear the cluttered worlds go up in smoke.

J. C.

Haiku

Two white birds
in a flash of winter sun
fly to meet in still water

Haiku

Wind ripples in the water—
I catch my breath—
the flying goose has flown

Haiku

A sudden night wind—
the dark vlei waters shiver:
sound of broken moon

B. F.

Clock Time

This house on the water:
sitting down to write at its table
I hear the cough of water-fowl, their wing-beats
amplified by water. Listen long enough,

and you too will taste this crisp knowledge
and forget the ticking of your watch.

And I, a weekend poet on the prowl here,
having silenced for an instant the syllables
that are forever marching through my brain—
what do I know?

I know by the stubble on my cheek
that I slept in a strange bed,
and called it mine; know by this ring I wear
that brightness grows slowly in the dark
before it shines; know by the sound of wing-beats
that I am animal also;
know that somehow inside
this rusty, tick-tock universe
you and I have stood listening out
into a slow stripping down,
till time and our minds stopped together.

J. C.

Tokai

My heart fills
with the sound of rain
and the forest
rattling its bones
—in the storm—

and I remember that wild afternoon
and the dogs mad with excitement—

and me with fear
of lightning
and branches falling—

and still we made
the whole circuit
of the wild wet wood—

filling ourselves with the rage of it.

B. F.

Autumn Drive

Everything is clear today:
the rocks along the railway are shining,
you say, and the wonder in your voice
is tangible.

I try to adjust an inner landscape
into something that could contain all this—
glimmering rock, pools of clear rain water
in puddles beside the road, a winter light.

But always in the end I turn instead
to you, and plunge my arms into your voice—
caressing its contours, the vast distances there.

J. C.

Your Bright Future

Last night I remembered
how I once wrote a poem to a young poet,
honouring the men of old—
men who laid the cornerstones
of cathedrals they would never see—how

they served their craft,
yet could but dream the greatness
of that future edifice. Last night,

in the small bookshop, I sat
listening (with the loved and fusty books,
floor to ceiling, all around me) listening
to a glimpse of a future I would never know;
listening to a voice,
a bright stone falling down an ancient well—

and far below, the hidden waters breaking
with a new and terrifying authority. Listening
to your Braille fingers stutter out
the clean-cut building-stones of your bright future—

and hearing my own mortality written
into every line.

B. F.

Switch

He knew he would always remember it like this:
half walking, half stumbling with her
through slow stretches of time—and then,

in the middle of nowhere,
suddenly it would be as if
a great light
had turned itself on in his mind—
and he would sit down next to her, unable to speak,

flooded with this astonishment,
wave upon helpless wave of it:

and outside there would be sun, or maybe rain,
or maybe it would be in a strange room—
it made no difference. He knew there would only ever be
this turning over of his senses,
and she next to him—utterly familiar,
utterly strange and new.

J. C.

Ode to Mystery

What mystery then, when all the measurements are done?
I pray the gods may scuttle all conclusions.

I can hold it in my hands—this skull; this house
of heaven and hell—this ivory cave made old with wind
and shadows, where images make play upon the walls,
and memory cradles her haunting song.

A work of centuries, this box of whisperings
and numinous emanations; this hermetic cell
of finite measure—yet holds an inner sky, wider than ever
I could dream it: infinity—vast, boundless. And terrifying.

This domed vessel of knitted bone resounds with intuitions
and superstitions, and dark penumbral imaginings;
and evil, and innocence, and small satisfactions—and
        greatness.
And deep within, the flower and fruit—the root of instinct.

All the seasons of the soul are gathered here, and histories
we have not yet recalled; and longing, and desire,
and death, and madness—
and a fierce black wind to blow the night sky
full of stars and mystery.

The beating of my heart brings metre
and measure to it.

And you are here—
and I—
and all eternity blowing through it.

B. F.

The Inner Work

I

This black stone,
dark jewel of many facets,
can tilt the hand that holds it;
can speak of dark matter, things invisible
except to a mind as hot
as the fire that it was forged in.

It is possible to burn
with a steady flame that can outlast the night,
but for that you must descend
into the liquid dark where it was made
in heat and silence.

II

I know that this golden
ring that we have chosen, a black
diamond set in it, holds
no promise of safety from
life and its small
or large betrayals. Yet,
sitting in this springtime room
almost entirely protected from the world,
because of it I dare to know
even this place as wilderness,

and this token of the slow
fires under the earth—
it is a magic circle we have drawn
around ourselves, meaning
an essential territory, meaning
a slow making that is shared.
O, wondrous crafting.

J. C.

Stone Cottage: West Coast

The silence in this stone cottage
is as old as the cave.

In the rough hearth,
white-wash and burnt clay; a fire
awakens a primitive connection.
Outside everything bends
to the rain.
The night is cold.

And the darkness cannot find us.

B. F.

Happy

One gets used to being happy,
like anything else. Slowly

you forget the miracle:
those dawns when you picked yourself up and swallowed
          the sun,
and shouted something untranslatable
into the open wind.

We sip coffee in the mornings now
to the accompaniment of slow, dark chords
that resonate far off like dormant volcanoes;
we know ourselves to be survivors, lucky.

And yet there is an edge to all this peace:
notice how these chords rumble against
the structures that would hold them.

And I, caught in what must be
the oldest gesture—pulling you
closer into me—know and say
too much about it. Never
facing the moment squarely, never
as the saying goes, out
of my mind.

J. C.

Afterword

This book emerged slowly out of joint poetry readings that Barbara Fairhead and I gave at Off the Wall, the long-standing poetry event that Hugh Hodge hosted in Observatory, Cape Town, for many years. When Barbara and I met in the winter of 2005, it was housed at A Touch of Madness, a quirky eating-house in Lower Main Road. The room that had been set aside for these gatherings was across the passage from a noisy bar, and often poets had to summon considerable breath and courage to make themselves heard.

Barbara and I were immediately drawn to each other, but for a time we were unsure what form our relationship should take. Writing some of these poems, and reading them out loud in front of an audience, was a way to simultaneously celebrate and contain powerful emotions that nevertheless got the better of us eventually.

On the night in December 2005, when we gave our first joint reading, something extraordinary happened in the room. We sat down at the same microphone, read two or three poems each, and then made room for the other to do the same. Many of the short poems we chose were explicitly in conversation with each other, but even older poems, written before we'd met, seemed to gather a new resonance. At first we thought that this resonance was something only we could feel, created by our recent memories of the events and emotions that inspired the poems in the first place, but over the years, as we repeated the experiment, we realised that our experience was shared by those who heard our poems in this context.

This collection, then, is an attempt to reproduce on the page the energy of those readings. Sometimes the dialogue between poems was intentional to begin with; sometimes the connections between them emerged slowly, over long stretches of life together. In the years since that first reading we have married, set up three different houses together, and released four albums of music under the name Red Earth & Rust.

The collection has been arranged in such a way that the two voices alternate symmetrically. For the sake of clarity, our initials appear at the bottom of each page.

We would like to thank Eduard Burle for his consummate editorial skills, and for his infinite patience in comparing different versions of the poems while they were in progress. We also want to thank the many readers and listeners who have encouraged us to believe that a collection such as this might have an audience.

Jacques Coetzee

About the authors

BARBARA FAIRHEAD was born in the UK in 1939, and has lived in South Africa since 1948. She is an artist, sculptor, fiction writer, and the lyricist for the band Red Earth & Rust. She has published two books of poetry: *And Now You Have Leapt Up To Swallow the Sun* (1997) and *Word and Bead: The*  *Presentation of a Journey* (2001). *Of Death and Beauty*, her first novel, was published in 2013 by Sunstone Press, Santa Fe, New Mexico. Its sequel, *Whereof One Cannot Speak*, will be published later in 2017.

JACQUES COETZEE matriculated from the Pioneer School for the Blind in Worcester. He completed a master's degree in creative writing at the University of Cape Town, for which he submitted a manuscript of poems called *Singing Through*. He has worked as a busker at the Cape Town Waterfront, and tutored English literature to first- and second-year university students. He is the singer and one of the main songwriters in the band Red Earth & Rust, which has released four albums of original songs to date.

Printed in the United States
By Bookmasters